T0146438

CLOSE YOUR TAB & DON'T LOOK BACK

CLOSE YOUR TAB & DON'T LOOK BACK

A Guide to Getting Out of Debt and Getting Ahead in the Real World

ANGELA OZAR

CLOSE YOUR TAB & DON'T LOOK BACK
A GUIDE TO GETTING OUT OF DEBT AND
GETTING AHEAD IN THE REAL WORLD

iUniverse books may be ordered through booksellers or by contacting:

iUniverse
1663 Liberty Drive
Bloomington, IN 47403
www.iuniverse.com
1-800-Authors (1-800-288-4677)

Because of the dynamic nature of the Internet, any web addresses or links contained in this book may have changed since publication and may no longer be valid. The views expressed in this work are solely those of the author and do not necessarily reflect the views of the publisher, and the publisher hereby disclaims any responsibility for them.

Any people depicted in stock imagery provided by Thinkstock are models, and such images are being used for illustrative purposes only. Certain stock imagery © Thinkstock.

ISBN: 978-1-5320-3450-3 (sc)
ISBN: 978-1-5320-3449-7 (e)

Library of Congress Control Number: 2017915308

Print information available on the last page.

iUniverse rev. date: 01/25/2018

DEDICATION

For God, who gave me everything I have in the first place. My dad, who taught me everything I know and believe about handling finances. And for the women graduating from college with debt and dreams, just like I did.

TABLE OF CONTENTS

PART I

PART II

LEGAL DISCLAIMER

This book is for informational purposes only. It is not a substitute for professional financial advice. The information and statistics mentioned in this book are current as of the last five years. Laws can change that would affect this information.

Personal Disclaimer

This book is written solely from my experience successfully managing my personal finances and paying off my student loan debt in three years. I realize that not everyone may be able to pay off their debt as quickly as I did, and that's OK. Everyone comes from a different financial situation and viewpoint, and each one is valid. No one's story is the same. My intent is to be helpful and to provide some practical tips and tricks for managing your finances and your life after college. Let me give you a little bit of background information.

As of 2016, the average college grad graduates with $37K in student loan debt.[1] When I graduated from college with my undergraduate degree, I had about $29K in student

---

[1] Powell, Farran. "10 Student Loan Facts College Grads Need to Know." *U.S. News*, May 9, 2016, www.usnews.com/education /best-colleges/paying-for-college/slideshows/10-student-loan-facts-college-grads-need-to-know.

loan debt. I was personally responsible for paying back my loan; my parents and my profession didn't help me. I had a student job all through college and I was wise with my spending and saving. By being the annoying overachiever in class, I worked my butt off to get a really good job right after school. I've never had debt from a credit card, and I don't plan on having any in the future. I disciplined myself to pay back my loan in a short amount of time, while investing in my future and avoiding any additional debt. If I didn't take the steps I did, then I wouldn't be sharing any of this with you.

Keep these things in mind while reading this book and don't get caught up in comparing your financial situation to mine. What's important is that you are seeking help to pay off your debt and managing your finances at such a critical point in your life.

Assumptions

I made some assumptions in presenting this information:

- Each individual is personally responsible for his or her financial future
- People reading this book have varying amounts of debt from college
- People reading this book are personally paying off that debt
- People reading this book have public government-held loans
- People reading this book aim to get jobs using their college educations to pay off their debt.

PREFACE

This book was written specifically for women, but men can learn from and enjoy this book, too. In my career, I have spoken with many women who couldn't start businesses or pursue their dreams because of the financial mistakes they made early on in their lives. This experience sparked me to share what I've learned so that young women could avoid these pitfalls. Aside from my personal experience, there are some other statistics that explain why this book is targeted towards women:

- There is an increasing number of women attending college across every ethnicity[2]
- 42% of women have more than $30K in student loan debt, 1.5x that of men at 27%[3]

---

[2] Lopez, Mark Hugo, and Ana Gonzalez-Barrera. "Women's College Enrollment Gains Leave Men Behind." *Pew Research Center*, March 6, 2014, www.pewresearch.org/fact-tank/2014/03/06/womens-college-enrollment-gains-leave-men-behind/.

[3] Dickler, Jessica. "College Debt Weighs More Heavily on Women than on Men." *CNBC*, CNBC, January 25, 2017, www.cnbc.com/2017/01/25/women-carry-bigger-burden-of-student-loan-debt-than-men.html.

- Women are 2x more likely than men to think it will take them more than the average amount of 20 years to pay off their debt[4]

These statistics show that we need to do a better job of preparing women (and men) to manage their student loan debt. My hope is that this book is a start.

---

[4] Dickler, "College Debt Weighs.."

ACKNOWLEDGEMENTS

First, I want to thank my editor and motivator, Caitlin Saia. She has made me a better writer, and without her help and encouragement, I never would have found my voice, or had the courage to publish this book. I also want to give credit (no pun intended) and a special thanks to Britt Scearce for being my expert source on all things credit. I want to thank my family and friends who encouraged me to write this book; especially my dad (and financial role model) for sharing all of his wisdom about money management and constantly asking me when I was going to become a published author. Special shout-outs to Michael Heckman, Kara Warden, Katie Denlinger, Debra Mooney, Brad Felix, Michael Winkfield, and Paige Klein, who supported me in special ways throughout this process. I also want to thank Caitlin's friends, and recent college grads, Katie Rankin and Matthew Murdock, who read my first draft and gave me unique feedback. Lastly, I would like to thank my 7th grade English teacher at Power Middle School who wrote, "You should write a book one day" on one of my papers. Without each and every one of you this book would not have become a reality.

INTRODUCTION

Every movie, every TV show, and even older relatives tell you that college is the best time of your life. They focus on the perks of college, like the constant partying, and how this will be the last time in your life that you will have no responsibilities. However, as a working adult, you still get to party (this is why happy hour was invented), but now you don't have homework and your bank account has a positive balance. So if you're grieving the fact that late nights and good times are seemingly behind you, consider the list below of the things you now have to look forward to after graduation day:

1. Say goodbye to your most dreaded day of the week, and say hello to #SundayFunday, because now you'll be at brunch instead of the library.
2. You'll lose weight (at least initially-see point 1) without even trying from the sheer lack of eating pizza and other refined carbohydrates daily.
3. You now get paid to go on vacation.
4. Visits to the doctor are now a treat because it means you get to leave work early.
5. Thursday night still feels like the beginning of the weekend, but now you have more money to cover your bar tab.

6. Weddings will soon take over your social calendar-free dinner, open bar, and partying like you never left college... what's not to like?
7. Who says 21 is the only milestone until 30? At 25 you can now rent a car without worrying that you'll be charged a fee.
8. You no longer get carded everywhere you go-especially if you're in business casual clothes at the grocery store after 5:00 p.m.
9. Your wardrobe gets upgraded from free t-shirts and school spirit wear.
10. Not only will you dress better, but you'll also be able to get your hair cut by a professional and more than twice a year.
11. Work travel is like taking a mini-vacation that you don't have to pay for.
12. You can now go back to reading books just for fun, as opposed to educational purposes.
13. You can now afford to get your friends and family actual Christmas and birthday presents that don't involve handmade cards or $5 coffee shop gift cards.

See? Your best days are yet to come, and they don't include cafeteria food, noise violations, or sleep deprivation.

Whether you have landed a job already, or you're still in the process, you are probably feeling a mix of emotions about graduating from college. It's totally normal to feel a concoction of emotions that will make you feel like a freshman all over again.

This book is designed to be a resource for you. As someone who has lived and learned, I'm here to help so that you don't have to relive those freshman memories in the professional world. Everything from information regarding your student loan, to which clothes you should have in your closet can be found in the following pages. Each chapter has a different theme that makes "adulting" a little more entertaining. You'll learn a strategy for paying off your loan ASAP, along with tools and tips to help you achieve this feat. You can skim, skip, or reference it, however, if you read it, you'll be better prepared than I was to conquer your finances and your life after college.

PART I

Start here if you don't have plans (AKA a job) after graduation day.

CHAPTER 1A

Financial Aspects of Finding a Job

The Search

The job search process, as well as the ultimate decision about where you want to work after school, are extremely important factors in determining your financial outlook. If you already have a job lined up after college, you can skim this section; if not, then continue reading.

You may have never thought you would end up on a reality dating show, but when looking for a job, your life will start to resemble one. It all starts with the search. Where do you go to find a job in your field, and how does an employer find you? This may surprise you, but your employer needs you as much as you need them. They are looking for the next star of their organization, and it's your job to prove to them that you're the one they have been looking for. It's just like you are auditioning to be on the next season of a dating show! Remember, it's also about finding the right fit for you, so they need to do some auditioning, too. If you don't know where to begin, take a look at the list for places you can find job postings. It won't be as obvious as a TV advertisement that says they are coming to a city near you, so it will require some effort and searching on your part.

Places to look:

- Organizational websites
- LinkedIn, Facebook, and other social media platforms
- Websites such as Indeed and Monster
- Networking (your parents, friends' parents, professors, etc.)
- Your school's career center job board

As you search, there is more to take into consideration than salary and location. If I have learned anything from watching years of reality TV shows about finding love, the key to a healthy, long-lasting relationship is finding someone who shares your interests and values. The same goes for the people you want to work with and for.

After you've found a few jobs that check the majority of your boxes, it's time to start applying. Don't worry, it won't require you needing a fresh blowout to record yourself on camera, but it will require you to customize your resume and cover letter for each specific organization and role. There is plenty of advice out there regarding writing resumes and cover letters, but my #1 suggestion is to use plenty of verbs and numbers when describing your previous work experience. Using verbs and numbers will demonstrate you are an engaged employee and will quantify your results. Ask your professors, the career center at your school, and even relatives and friends for more advice -especially if they are in your industry. They will have years of knowledge and experience that you can benefit from. Be careful not to get too much advice though, because everyone will have a different opinion and that can get overwhelming. In the end, trust your gut and make sure you're happy and confident with how you will be relaying your accomplishments on paper. And if all else fails, use your Googling skills that got you through school- Google always pulls through.

The Waiting Game

If you thought the hardest part about the job search process was clicking "Save As..." on your resume 50 times, you may be surprised to find the hardest part is actually waiting for a response. I know you've had some experience with this from waiting to hear back from people on your dating apps, but it doesn't make it any easier!

As you obsessively check your email and scramble to answer your phone when an unknown number pops up on the screen, it'll become obvious that your life will have more than enough material to fill a 12-episode TV show. While you wait, remain productive and clear your head. You can start shopping for a power pantsuit, printing copies of your resume on quality paper, and removing the chipped nail polish lingering on your nails.

The Selection

When you FINALLY get that call of a lifetime, you should feel confident enough to don that pantsuit; out of thousands of resumes, you made it in the "yes" pile. Now the next challenge is to make it past round one. In order to do that, you'll have to make a good first impression. Careful not to trip getting out of your ~~limo~~ used car when you arrive to your interview! It's normal to be nervous, and if you prepare properly, your nerves will fade away in the first few minutes and you'll go into autopilot.

Give your matches a break and use your energy to online stalk the companies with which you are interviewing. Of course, take note of their values, mission, etc., but also take a good look at the financial benefits they offer. This will come into play later as you successfully make it through round after round to the final offer ceremony. The more you know and are able to communicate, the more impressed your audience will be by your due diligence. Trust me, they'll be flattered- not freaked out- that you Googled them.

Channel your nervous energy into practicing for your interview. If you've practiced responding to interview questions and prepared your responses, the more confident you'll be, and the less likely you'll be to get flustered during your one-on-one. Most organizations use the STAR interview method, which stands for Situation, Task, Action, and Result. Your interviewer will want you to answer questions using the STAR method, so recall a few situations where you shone during your summer job or internship.

Make sure to follow through with what you did specifically to earn "Employee of the Month" at the dairy shack. For example, you could say: "I came up with a marketing idea to give free ice cream cones to kids under the age of five during the summer. After that, monthly sales increased over the last year by 15%." Numbers help here, so throw them in wherever possible to quantify the impact that you made. It's more than OK to brag about yourself here, so don't hold back! While you're retelling your summer at the dairy shack, you can also describe how you performed under pressure to manage the team when the line was out the door with families wanting ice cream. See what I did there? I used the same experience to answer another interview question so they can see how you handle stressful situations. Sort of like on the hometown date when you meet the parents for the first time.

The One-on-One

While you are doing your research and preparing for the interview, be sure to take good notes and write down questions you can ask later in the one-on-one. Bring your notes with you to the interview and pull them out when your interviewer says, "Do you have any questions about the position?" They will be expecting you to have questions, so blow them away by showing them you thought ahead. Unfortunately, you can't do this on a date, so take advantage of this rare occasion! This not only makes you look prepared and interested in the company, but it is also like taking an open-note exam. If you are having trouble thinking of questions, you can find sample questions online (thanks again, Google).

Since the focus of this book is setting you up for financial success after school, I have listed some sample questions you can ask regarding financial benefits, because unlike on a second date, during the second interview or later, you can (and should) talk about money. If you don't know what some of these terms mean, that is why glossaries were invented. You can look up the bolded words in the back of the book, along with some frequently asked questions that may be keeping you up at night after the graduation parties are over.

- Do they offer **401(k)** matching? If so, how much, and up to what amount per year?
- If they do offer a **Pension Plan**, what are the details?
- Do they have an **Employee Stock Purchase Plan**?
- Are there any other financial benefits they offer that set them apart?
- How long does it take to be **fully vested**?*

An organization may offer some other financial benefits to their employees that are non-traditional, like a vehicle or student loan repayment assistance. Wouldn't it be nice if more organizations offered to help you pay back part of your loan as a benefit? Who knows, it could be the future because it's gaining popularity as the "hottest new benefit."[5] In the meantime, we'll call these type of benefits, "perks." Keep these in mind when considering your job options. Financial perks will be unique to the company or industry. For example, if you're in sales, an employer might pay your cell phone bill, so you don't have to worry about being in a WiFi zone when you're swiping left and right on all your dating apps. It's

---

* Be careful with this one, as it is implying leaving the company after a short amount of time- and employers are not worried about that AT ALL (yeah, right). However, you do want to know this information, in case you decide to leave in the future.

[5] Friedman, Zack. "Student Loan Repayment: The Hottest Employee Benefit Of 2017." *Forbes*, Forbes Magazine, February 2, 2017, www.forbes.com/sites/zackfriedman/2016/12/19/student-loan-repayment-benefit/#2f892271d6fe.

not quite celebrity status, but these types of perks save you money now, as opposed to saving it in the future. We'll come back to this later when you've received your offer(s) of employment and are measuring them up.

Below is a list of perks that organizations may offer:

- Tuition reimbursement
- Company vehicle and free fuel
- Gym membership
- Monthly phone bill reimbursement or a discount at a cell phone carrier
- Discount at retail locations
- Student loan repayment assistance
- Extended paid maternity or paternity leave

The Final Round

After a few successful one-on-ones, you've made it through multiple cuts and there are only a few of you left vying for the opportunity. Before you go day dreaming about a flight to a remote island for an overnight stay, you need to focus. Now they know you, so show them why they should choose you.

During your final one-on-one, close the deal with some final questions that will make it impossible for them to say no to you. Here are a couple examples:

"Based on our conversations, is there any reason why you think I wouldn't be the perfect fit for this role?"

OR, if that pantsuit has you on a power trip, try something like:

"Out of the other candidates interviewing for this position,

I am confident that I am the right candidate for it for the following reasons… Do you agree?"

These questions will feel awkward saying aloud, but what they do is pull out any possible reasons a company may be hesitant to offer you the role. As long as they are truthful, getting them to tell you their concerns about hiring you is powerful because then you have the chance to address those concerns head on.

After you've effectively closed the interview, follow-up within the next 24 hours- just like your matches should if they are interested. When it comes to dating, handwritten thank you notes, calls, and emails may be enough to file a restraining order, but in the process of interviewing for a job, it's perfectly acceptable and expected. Take the time to make your thank you notes personal and sincere, without being over the top (hearts dotting the "i" and pink gel pen- those tactics worked in grade school but they won't work here).

By asking closing questions and following-up, you've done your job to prove to them that you're the one they have been searching for. If you don't get a final offer, you can have peace of mind knowing that it's most likely not you, it's them. Keep trying, because just like on a reality TV show, this isn't the end of the road for you. Those who don't get a rose at the end of the show almost always get to be the next leading lady or are featured on a spin-off.

The Final Offer Ceremony

Whether it's now or later, when you do get that offer of a lifetime, it's time to negotiate your terms, and, of course, celebrate your success.

Before you go celebrating the fact that your life is never going to be the same again, there is still one final detail. Now that you will have a "real job," you are most likely going to be off the hourly wage and onto salary. Well, how do you navigate the question of salary? And, should you negotiate your final offer?

First, you need an offer with a salary figure before you have anything to negotiate. This can get tricky, much like on a date if they bring up money. During the last part of the interview, the interviewer may try to ask about your salary requirements. Know that you do not have to answer. In fact, you shouldn't answer, but you also shouldn't avoid the question. Put the ball back in his or her court by saying, "If you tell me the salary range for the position, I can then tell you if that fits in my requirements." Crisis avoided.

In every negotiation, each side is usually thinking about themselves, and neglecting to consider the other person's point of view. The key to everyone winning, just like in any relationship, is listening for what the other person wants. In this case, they have already said that they want you, so you have every right to negotiate your total compensation package if you so choose. It can be intimidating, but keep in mind, the guys in your class are most likely negotiating for a higher salary, so you can, too. Each situation is different, though, so seek out trusted advice, turn to Google again, and ultimately go with your gut. Whether you negotiate your total compensation package or not, you have nothing to lose and everything to gain.

If you happen to be lucky enough to get more than one offer, compare and contrast their benefit packages. This will make it easier for you to choose between a few organizations.

Remember those perks we talked about earlier? Be sure to include those, too. Open up your spreadsheet, and bust out your data skills by making a simple chart like the one below.

	401(k)	Pension Plan	ESPP	Tuition Reimbursement	Perks
Company 1	Yes, $1 match	No	Yes	Yes, $2,500 per semester	$80 towards monthly phone bill
Company 2	Yes, $.50 match	No	No	Yes, $7,000 per year	Gym membership- $40 monthly value

Consider financial benefits as a part of your total compensation- and remember they are all up for negotiation. It won't seem as important as a cool office or free-breakfast-Fridays now, but later, when you are able to retire early, you'll be thanking yourself.

Estimate the dollar value of the financial benefit or perk(s) the company offers and add it to your starting salary. You could also calculate the value over time by using some quick formulas. Thought you'd never use those, right? This will help you see the true impact of these benefits on your finances.

In the end, choose the company that feels right to you. Seeking advice from family, friends, and your professors can be helpful, but it's your choice to make. You need to be happy with your choice because, after all, you're the one who is going to live with your decision day in and day out. So make sure you love them, because there will be days when you don't feel like giving them 100%, but you still have to work anyway.

The After Show

Now that you have found "the one" and have accepted a position, what can you expect? Call your cell phone carrier and upgrade your data plan because your new employer will be blowing up your phone with lots of important information about what comes next. Much of this information will be time sensitive, so check your messages daily and respond in a timely manner. This is not the time to act cool and respond eight hours later. Your mind may be in la la land, but it's not an excuse to drop your responsibilities or your ability to impress your new employer.

I suggest you get an organizational process in place for all of the letters you'll be receiving with important information you need to know, like when you can enroll in health benefits. Even though most things are done online now, it's still good practice to print the truly important documents. You can buy a portable filling system and create folders labeled with categories such as utilities, health benefits, housing, and **IRA** (you should definitely have one of these, look it up in the back if you're not familiar with the acronym). Keeping things organized during the transition will decrease your stress levels. As I am sure you know, or can imagine, it will be challenging to navigate the ups and downs of life post-college.

Going through the job search and interview process is grueling and drama-filled, but it's a rite of passage that everyone experiences. By taking my advice and doing your homework, you'll be prepared to shine when it truly matters. Once you receive the offer you've been waiting for, it will make all of the work and waiting worth it.

PART II

Start here if your plans after graduation day include sleeping in until the start date for your new job.

PART II

CHAPTER 1B

Understanding Your Loan by The Numbers

The Last First Day

You've been here before: the infamous first day. You have a dozen of them under your belt with the pictures to prove it. Now it's your first day on the job, the last first day for a while (maybe forever, and thank goodness your mom is not there with her phone to snap a pic). However, unlike your mom, those first day jitters don't go away. Will my boss like me? Will I make friends? Who will I eat with at lunch? Whose desk will be next to mine? It's both exciting, and nerve-wracking.

There will always been some unknown variables when you start something new, but it helps to have a friend or two by your side as you navigate through all of the uncertainty. Sort of like your freshman year roommate in the dorms, you'll be stuck with the people you work with, so it's important that you make them your friends and not your enemies.

It's important to have friends outside of work, too, because your work environment can change quickly. People get promoted, transferred, or quit, and suddenly, you may find yourself needing a new lunch buddy. That's the not-so-great part about having all of your friends be at your place of employment: they can be temporary.

While having friends from work to hang out with is a nice benefit of being a working adult, it can also be annoying when you want to escape from work. You end up talking about work all the time, even outside of the office at happy hour, because that's what you have in common with each other. I learned this lesson first hand: it's equally important to have friends inside and *outside* of work. However, I wish I could tell you it was easy as it was in college.

Friends Wanted

Why isn't it easy? Well, thanks to the digital age, it makes it a little more challenging to meet people outside of work when people are making eye contact with their screens instead of you. I wish the BFF setting on dating apps had been around during the many nights I sat alone in my apartment drinking wine and watching TV. In college, meeting people was as easy as stepping out of your dorm room, or being assigned a group project. In the real world, I have learned that it's a lot harder to make friends than at a college party. Chances are, even if you are staying in the same city after graduating, your friends are not. I bet you're wishing right now that you had taken a class on how to talk to random strangers instead of a second language. Yeah, me too. Luckily for you, I've been where you are, and have made friends. So I'll share my secrets of how to make friendships in the real world.

The secret to making friends is to get out and try some new things in your city. Finding recreation leagues, checking out young professional events, or attending a workout class at the gym can lead you to making new friends you won't see at work. You'll find things you like to do, and people who will do them with you. If you're checking Meetup.com and your Facebook event page more than your Instagram feed, you'll eventually find a group where you belong.

Debt is Not Your Friend

You'll make new friends after school; however, debt is one friend you don't want to have. I repeat: *debt is not your friend*. This seems obvious, but did you know 80% of Americans are living with debt?[6] Not to mention, the national student loan debt is $1.2 trillion and climbing at a rate of $2.7K per second.[7] You are at an ideal point where you can be one out of every five Americans living a debt-free life. All you need to do is learn from me, and pay off your student loan, without racking up any more debt.

You'll have to repay your loan one way or another. You can either spend more time and money doing it, or take my advice (which I strongly suggest). Don't listen to the mainstream message about debt. You don't have all the time

---

[6] *The Complex Story of American Debt*. Report. July 2015. www. pewtrusts.org/~/media/assets/2015/07/reach-of-debt-report_artfinal. pdf?la=en.

[7] Berman, Jillian. "America's Student-Loan Debt Growing $2,726 Every Second." *MarketWatch*, January 30 2016, www.marketwatch. com/story/every-second-americans-get-buried-under-another-3055-in-student-loan-debt-2015-06-10.

in the world to pay it off. In fact, *you cannot afford to delay your student loan repayment.*

It takes the average student loan borrower 21 years to repay their debt. 21 years,[8] which means by the time you are free from your student loan, you'd be 43 (and I've heard, half your life is practically over past 40). By the age of 43, you will most likely have more debt. You'll have a mortgage payment, probably a car payment, and not to mention kids -which have a whole price tag of their own. So that means, at the very minimum, you would spend nearly a quarter of your life not having the freedom to spend your money the way you want. Listen to someone who is living life debt-free and ignore the mainstream message about debt. Don't take your time paying back your student loan. Your dreams are too big, and your life (and your money) is too important to not be able to spend it how you want.

Math: Friend or Foe?

If the acronym **FAFSA** sounds vaguely familiar, or gave you a major headache at the beginning of each year, it's safe to assume that you have a loan from the federal government. There are a few types of Federal Student Loans. It's important to know which type of loan you have, because they have different grace periods and, in some cases, different interest rates. I've listed three steps that will help you understand

---

[8] Bidwell, Allie. "Student Loan Expectations: Myth vs. Reality." *U.S. News & World Report*, U.S. News & World Report, October 7, 2014, www.usnews.com/news/blogs/data-mine/2014/10/07/student-loan-expectations-myth-vs-reality.

your loan type, the repayment plans that are available, and how to calculate interest on your loan.

Step 1: Identify which loan you have. The different types are listed below:

- **Direct Subsidized Loan**
- **Direct Unsubsidized Loan**
- **Direct PLUS Loan**
- **Federal Perkins Loan**

For the purpose of this book, we'll focus on Federal Subsidized and Unsubsidized Loans, also known as Stafford Loans,[9] because these are the most common.

If you thought you could get away with not paying back your loan, like you did with your parents growing up, think again. *You have to pay back your student loan -even if you didn't finish your education.* The good news is that you may have some time after graduation to make a plan for paying it back. This is called a **grace period**; isn't the government so nice? There are a few exceptions to this rule, like if you are joining the military, going back to school before the period ends, or you **consolidate** your loans.[10] Super seniors think they have the right idea, but more school = more debt.

Upon graduation, you will have the option of setting up a student loan repayment plan. If you have a Direct Subsidized or Unsubsidized Loan, you have the grace

---

[9] Onink, Troy. "Use These 8 Loans To Pay For College." *Forbes*, Forbes Magazine, June 1, 2016, www.forbes.com/sites/troyonink/2013/01/22/use-these-8-loans-to-pay-for-college/2/.

[10] "How to Repay Your Loans." *Federal Student Aid*, last modified July 30, 2017, studentaid.ed.gov/sa/repay-loans.

period of six months to choose a plan. Don't get too excited, though, because in most cases, interest will accrue during the grace period. There are several plans to choose from, and an overview of all of the options can be found on the Federal Student Aid (FSA) office website (www.studentaid.ed.gov). The plans range from allowing yourself up to 25 years to pay back your loan, to being income-based, and letting you pay as you earn.

Step 2: Set up your repayment plan.

If you don't choose a plan (aka do nothing), you will automatically be placed on the Standard Repayment Plan. Similar to claiming your co-workers as friends, it's the default mode. On the Standard Repayment Plan, it will take you ten years to pay off - that is, if you pay the minimum payment due each month. Ten years is the minimum repayment plan option that the FSA office recognizes. They want a long-term friendship with you; however, you don't want a long-term friendship with them.

The US. Department of Education (parent to the FSA office) has **loan servicers** that they use to collect your loan. They are the middle man, and you'll be dealing with them to pay back your loan.

In the following chapters, I'll share my strategy for paying off my loan in the first three years after graduating from college. By following the steps I took and adopting my spending (and saving) hacks during your first few years out of college, you'll pay off your student loan in a lot shorter time period than ten years.

In case you need any more reasons as to why you should

pay off your student loan ASAP (or slept through business finance class), let's go over a few math problems. I know you thought you were done with school and would never have to see a mathematical formula ever again; but, in case your professors didn't tell you, math problems could save you thousands of dollars over the course of your lifetime.

When you graduate and get your bill, you'll realize there is also a price to pay for having a good time, and it's not just a killer hangover. There is a fee added onto your total, or in other terms: **interest.** Talk about a buzz kill. Interest rates vary by loan type and the date the loan is **dispersed.** The rates are set by Congress, so you can either blame them or thank them for your interest rate. In addition to interest, depending on which type of loan you have, you may also have incurred a fee for the total loan. This means the amount of money you received was actually lower than the amount you borrowed. When you pay back your loan, you are responsible for paying back the entire amount of the loan, not just the amount of money you actually received.

By doing some quick math, you will see how much you will spend in interest if you complete your plan by paying the minimum monthly payment. If this doesn't motivate you to pay back your loan in faster than ten or 20 years, I don't know what will.

Step 3: Find your interest rate and do some math (you can find this either on the FSA website or in a letter from your loan servicer).

I'll use my loan and repayment plan as an example. My original **principal**= $28.8K.

Standard Plan monthly loan payment = $332.95
Number of payments= 120
Interest rate= 6.8% (Congress wasn't kind that year)
Total amount owed (if I were a rule- follower) = $39K

By subtracting the principal balance from the total amount with interest over the completion of the plan, I discovered I would have paid a little over $11,000 in interest if I would have waited to pay back my loan over the course of ten years. That's a little over a $1,000 a year in interest, or an annual beach getaway. Now, I did pay some interest on my loan, but I saved myself about $8,000 by paying off my loan in just under three years. Remember- the average American takes 21 years to pay off their student loan.[11] So, how much would I have paid in interest if I had taken 21 years to pay off my loan? I don't even want to do that math.

My loan servicer was kind enough to include the total amount I would owe, including interest, at the current rate for my loan. All I had to do was some simple subtraction (to determine the total amount of interest I would have paid), some division (to get the amount of interest per year), and some multiplication (to see how much I saved myself in interest by paying it off in two and half years instead of ten). If your loan servicer did not provide you with this information, don't worry, I'll tell you how to figure it out for yourself.

The FSA office uses the simple daily interest formula to calculate interest. It is your outstanding principal balance x the # of days since last payment x the interest rate factor.

---

[11] Bidwell, Allie. "Student Loan Expectations: Myth vs. Reality."

The **Interest Rate Factor** is used to calculate the amount of interest that accrues on your loan. It is determined by dividing your loan's interest rate by the number of days in the year. Sound confusing? It is.

If you are more in the camp of "that's why calculators were invented," go online to the FSA office website and use their calculator (Repayment Estimator) to see how much you would pay with each plan. I am here to help, so I provided you with an example. I used the average student debt for a four-year public university-according to the FSA website ($26,946) with the current interest rate (3.9%) at the time of this book being published. I also plugged in the average starting salary for a college grad in 2016 ($50,000)[12] in the "Income Estimator."

Estimate Your Payments

Your Loan Information

○ Use Your Loans

◉ Use Average Loan Balances

| 4-year, Public | ∨ |

The balance below represents the average total federal student loan balance of a student at a 4-year public school has upon graduation.

Average Loan Balance $26,946

Interest Rate   3.9 %

More Information

Your Tax Filing Status

Select your tax filing status:

| Single | ∨ |

---

[12] "Student Loan Repayment Estimator." *Repayment Estimator*, studentloans.gov/myDirectLoan/mobile/repayment/repaymentEstimator.action#view-repayment-plans.

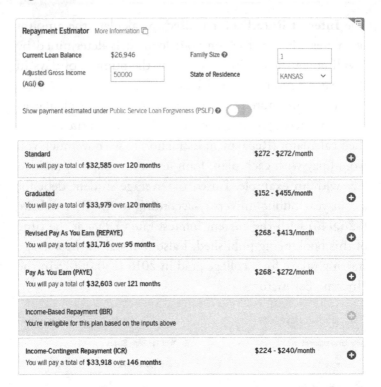

I used the same tool again, but plugged in my information from my loan. This is my output: I would have paid 1.5X my original principal if I had chosen any other plan and taken the full amount of time to repay my loan.

Repayment Plan	First Monthly Payment	Last Monthly Payment	Total Amount Paid	Projected Loan Forgiveness ❶	Repayment Period
Standard ❶	$332	$332	$39,798	$0	120 months
Graduated ❶	$191	$574	$42,825	$0	120 months
Revised Pay As You Earn (REPAYE) ❶	$227	$451	$43,090	$0	135 months
Pay As You Earn (PAYE) ❶	$227	$332	$43,542	$0	145 months
Income-Based Repayment (IBR) ❶	-	-	-	-	-
IBR for New Borrowers ❶	$227	$332	$43,542	$0	145 months
Income-Contingent Repayment (ICR) ❶	$265	$293	$43,569	$0	154 months

I wish we lived in a world where there were more positive examples of people paying off debt and living freely. However, that's not reality. But like me, you can be part of the 20% of Americans living debt free if you take aggressive strides to pay off your student loan.[13] It's not exactly the most popular route, but in the end, it has the best payoff-both on your wallet and on your life choices. So to recap:

Step 1: Identify which loan you have.
Step 2: Set up your repayment plan (I recommend the Standard 10-year Plan).
Step 3: Find your interest rate and do some math (you can find this either on the FSA website or in a letter from your loan servicer).

Once you've completed these steps, you will have refreshed your math skills, and you'll be on your way to paying back your student loan. You can start picking out your vacation destination knowing how much money you'll have saved yourself by paying off your debt in faster than ten years' time. Besides, I heard it's ten years later that the popular kids in school find themselves being shown up by the not-so-popular ones from class. Now that's something to cheers to at happy hour with friends.

---

[13] *The Complex Story of American Debt.* Report. July 2015.

CHAPTER 2

Saving, Spending & Credit

No Guac = Vacation Sooner

You may be confused about how I got there; after running the numbers on your student loan plan, you should be able to solve that simple equation. See, wasn't that algebra class worth the $30,000 price tag? Read on to learn why it matters that you say "no" to the extra charge for now, so you can splurge later once you are debt-free. It's time to get serious for a minute, so you can understand how being debt-free could affect your life beyond getting a killer tan.

My Story
Two Months after Graduation Day

Corporate job? Check. Company car? Check. On my way to climbing the career ladder to success? Check. I had landed the "dream" job right after college, while most of my friends and peers were either getting ready to do their victory lap in college or were scrambling to get a job after school. All of my boxes were checked and I was ready to take on the world.

Three Years Later

A few years at my corporate job was enough for me. I was bored and unhappy, so I started a new journey to find my purpose in life- in true Millennial fashion- and that lead me to voluntarily uncheck those boxes. I decided to leave my corporate job that provided me with job stability and financial security and take a leap of faith. I would soon find out what happens when a person can do what they love because of smart financial choices.

Today

I work at my dream job. One that offers no benefits, no career paths, and a much lower salary. I couldn't be happier. I'm not sure what comes next, but I'm on what was promised to be an adventure- an adventure that helps women in entrepreneurship.

I have personally helped and encouraged over 100 women start and grow their businesses. I have met hundreds of inspiring people who are making a difference in the lives of these women and in their communities. I've helped rebuild and rebrand an organization to expand its mission. An adventure I was promised, and an adventure is what I got.

One leap of faith made a difference for me personally, and in my career. I want you to experience this, too: to experience what it feels like to not be limited by financial burden, and to do what you want to do in life.

What things do you want to do? What dreams do you have? What does being debt-free mean to you? Know your why, and remind yourself of it every time you see your bank account take a nose dive; we'll talk more about this later. I don't want you to let your debt hold you back from doing what you love and enjoying your life.

How to Save After Reselling Your Textbooks

Hopefully, my story has inspired you to splurge on your payments to the government instead of the guac. You just never know when being debt-free might come in handy. Not only will it make your parents and alma mater proud, but it also means you can ditch the guilt and eat chips and guac in Mexico sooner, rather than in a restaurant resembling a tin can with a view of the parking lot. Sounds like a win-win. Now that's a math equation you can appreciate, so save up your vacation days and follow these tips and tricks on where to spend and save right after you get your diploma.

Live on a Dollar Beer Night Budget

The best advice I can give anyone about how to spend money after college is *to spend money like you're still in college.* Yes, you read that right. I know, I know, that is probably not what you wanted to hear. I'm sure you were so looking forward to upgrading your meals from Asian noodles and PB & J, and you will be able to do that eventually, just not right away. Why? Well, just because you are now making a salary that has three zeros added to what you made at your part-time job in college, doesn't mean you have that income just yet. Accumulating wealth takes time; it takes spending frugally, while saving aggressively. You will not have earned your new total salary until your one-year work anniversary, so don't go spending like you have that money in the bank before you've even earned it yet. Moral of the story: your spending habits shouldn't change overnight just because you're making more money than you did waiting tables in school.

Even though you're not living on campus, I suggest you not only keep your diet of mac and cheese, but also your college budgeting mindset and your acquired taste for cheap beer. Trust me and skip the $10 beers and specialty cocktails. Believe it or not, being partial to cheap beer can help speed up your student loan repayment, so keep those happy hour specials and $1 beer nights on your calendar. Yes, your hangovers may be worse, but your dollar will stretch much further- and this doesn't apply just to going out. Use the college budget part of your brain to apply this thinking to every other spending category. You've had four or five years (hopefully not more) of practice, so this should come as naturally as hitting the snooze button every morning. For instance, keep buying the store brand peanut butter; your PB & J will taste the same, if not better, because you saved $2. You may not think that saving $2 on a jar of peanut butter is going to help you pay off your student loan, but saving $2 here and there adds up over a long period of time. It's the little choices you make each day about how you spend your money that will set you up for financial success or failure.

Sit on Your Savings

Literally. Sit on the money you've saved by using second-hand stuff, Swedish furniture, and online steals. For me, the majority of my belongings came from my grandparents and "shopping" at my parent's house. This did mean I got to skip out on the confusing picture directions, but it also meant that I was sitting on my grandmother's hideous, floral print couch.

Well, fast forward five years later and I still own many of those hand-me-downs that I hated at the time. I replaced some items, but to both your and my surprise, the hideous, floral print couch still remains. The hideous couch I still hate, but, hey, couch covers exist for a reason! I'd like to thank the man who invented that wonderful creation because now my couch and debt are covered, and I can spend money on clothes and vacations. Ask yourself, would you rather sit on the beach with your best friend or on a leather sectional? I'm hoping it's the former, and if you want to achieve that, resist the urge to spend money on all new stuff just because you're excited about your new life.

Buying everything new when you're first starting out isn't the wisest choice. That is the first mistake many post-grads make. They want everything new, and everything right now. I promise, you don't need a fancy mixer with all of the attachments to make PB & J, and you have your whole life to own a brand-new, leather sectional- you don't need one right now. Besides, it's bound to have beer spilled on it anyway. One day, I'll invest some money into quality home furnishings, and you can, too. Until then, sit on your savings, follow your dollar beer night budget, and spend your money on things you'll actually want to buy. Choose wisely, though, because mac and cheese does get old very quickly.

So cheap happy hours, cheap furniture, plus the cheap peanut butter = a life like you're living on vacation, free from student loan debt. Cheap is the key word here and you know it well from your college days. This formula will help you pay back your loan, eventually allowing you to go on that vacation.

The Times When You Can and Should Get the Guac (aka upgrades)

Buy New Clothes and the Guac

So far, we have covered ways to save money when you're first starting out, and traps to avoid, like overspending your new salary before your first day on the job. All of this information is necessary preparation for establishing your financial success. Now, we're going to transition to what you should buy and how you should pay for it.

You may not believe what I'm about to tell you, but go and buy yourself some new clothes. Yes, *invest in your closet.* Your uniform of yoga pants and a hoodie for the last four years doesn't exactly scream "career driven young professional"- unless you happen to be in a medical profession, which essentially allows you to wear sweats to work. For all of you who don't fit into that category, having a new job where you need to look and act your best every day is reason enough to invest in yourself, and your wardrobe.

When I first graduated from college, clothes were the first thing I upgraded in my life. I knew shopping at the same stores I did throughout college wouldn't pass the test. A) They didn't sell anything that could be remotely deemed "work appropriate" and B) being sewn somewhere in a far off land and made of cheap material meant that they probably wouldn't make it to the end of the year without being ruined. Do yourself a favor and shop for some quality clothes, clothes that you wouldn't wear to a night club and clothes you might have hanging in your closet years later. But, don't think this is a free pass to have a total makeover and give your credit card a work out. For now, leave the low quality rating to the beer and get some high-quality wardrobe staples. The key word here is staples, not wardrobe.

You'll benefit from this list I put together to help get you started. After years of experience dressing for the professional world, I've noticed that these are the items I find myself constantly reaching for in the morning when I'm struggling to get out of bed:

- A black blazer
- 2 pairs of heels (one black and one in a pattern or fun color)
- 1 pencil skirt
- 2 pairs of flats (one nude and one black)
- 2 pairs of comfortable, but appropriate, dress pants (one black and one in another color)
- 2 blouses
- 1 cardigan (black, grey, or cream)
- 1 dress (LBD is always a good choice)

With this list of wardrobe basics, you'll have enough options to make multiple work outfits for weeks. For example:

1. Blouse + pencil skirt + heels (fun color)
2. Pants + blouse + blazer + heels
3. Dress + blazer + flats

4. Pants + blouse + cardigan + flats

Who said math couldn't be fun? And just like your hand-me-down couch, mac and cheese diet, and taste for cheap beer- this won't last forever. As you continue to earn money and get closer to becoming debt-free, fill in the gaps with the non-essentials and accessories to add your own flair. It takes time, but before you know it, you'll find your style. By only buying the essentials now, it will also give you some time to determine what you really need, so you're not going out wasting your money on items you'll never wear. Just hang on to that college mindset for a few more years, and after your debt is paid off, you can finally let that mindset go (along with the boxed dinners and cheap drinks).

Give Yourself a Little Credit, but Not Before You Pay Your Dues

When you're out shopping for these clothes and the nice lady at the store offers you an additional 20% off your bill for signing up for their company's credit card, stay strong and say NO. It will be tempting to get a card from your favorite clothing store in order to get a better discount, but trust me, you'll be doing yourself more damage than good. The **APR** (Annual Percentage Rate aka interest rate) is outrageous compared to a standard **credit card** you would get at your bank. And do you really need another temptation for buying that dress you know you should wait to buy until it's 50% off? I didn't think so. So skip the lure of discounts for a VIP pass to a lifetime of credit card debt- if you don't, you'll find yourself in need of a different retail therapy.

Delay getting a credit card until you have paid off your debt. Manage one form of debt at a time! I didn't get a credit card until the year I paid off my student loan debt. I only got one as a precaution for traveling internationally, just in case I was stranded in a third world country without the local currency. Luckily, I didn't end up needing it. This is how you should treat credit: only for emergencies. In case I need to clarify, a 50% off sale does not count as an emergency. There is an exception to this rule and we'll get to that in a second, so if you already have a credit card or multiple, that's OKAY and don't cancel it. It's better to use them and pay the monthly balance than to cancel them completely. As my credit expert, Britt Scearce from my local credit union says, "When applying for new credit it is the length of time your accounts have been established, which accounts for 15% of your **FICO**® (credit) score, so it is best to keep your existing accounts open as long as possible."

If you don't currently have a credit card, but think you may need one, or people are advising you to get one, here are some questions to ask yourself (answer them honestly):

1. Are you planning on buying a house in a few years?
2. Do you have addictions? Or an addictive personality?
3. Do your parents or guardians have credit card debt?
4. Can you trust yourself to pay the monthly balance?
5. Are you planning on doing a lot of international travel?
6. Would having a credit card make you feel more secure?
7. Do you have a lot of self-discipline?

8. Do you want a credit card, or do you want a discount or airline miles?

There are no right answers to these questions, but here are my suggestions:

If you are planning on purchasing a house in a few years, then it would be a good idea to start building credit now. Why? Because, unlike your landlords in college, your bank will want to know you are responsible enough to pay your mortgage. Credit history is a good way for them to see if they can trust you, based on your prior experience handling money that you owe.

If you can trust yourself to use a credit card and only make purchases you can afford so you can pay off the monthly balance, then go ahead and get one – just one, and make sure it's not a store card. If you are planning on doing a lot of international travel (and you should be!), and it would make you feel more secure to have a credit card for emergency situations, then it would also be a good idea for you to get a credit card.

On the other hand, if you have addictive tendencies, it may not be a good idea to get a credit card. These behaviors can affect your financial stability and can translate into other areas of your life, such as your relationship with credit. Addictions to shopping, smoking, gambling, drinking, beauty treatments, etc. can get you into financial trouble if they are supported by your credit card. Be honest with yourself, and if you can't trust yourself not to get carried away, then it's not a good idea to get a credit card. Lastly, if your parents or guardians have credit card debt, it is <u>not </u>a determining factor that you will; however, just like you inherited the ability to quickly (or not) metabolize all that junk food in college, our parents and guardians have a strong influence on our thoughts and behaviors when it comes to money. Keep that in mind before you make your decision about getting a credit card.

Now you can feel confident passing on the guac from time to time and sticking with the cheap beer, knowing it's for a good cause. You can save yourself money by saving in the right areas, like sitting on your used stuff, and in turn, spend money on things you need for your new life and that you'll actually enjoy. Say "Bon Voyage" to your student loan debt and "Hola" to the benefits of making good financial choices.

CHAPTER 3

Repaying Your Loan ASAP

Your Plan to Repayment

At this point, you might be daydreaming about sipping a margarita on the beach and have a craving for Mexican food, but don't let your brain go into vacation mode just yet- you've still got some work to do in order to earn the debt-free life. Whatever motivates you to get out of your student debt, whether it a vacation on the beach, or being able to change careers, remember your end goal while you plan- the palm trees will come later.

After you graduate, you have six months to make your first payment towards your student loan. If you graduated in the spring like I did, that means by November you'll be saying "Happy Holidays" to the federal government with a nice chunk of change. I know you were planning to buy your mom a nice watch for Christmas, but trust me, she'll be just as happy with a candle, especially if she knows you're thinking about your financial future so someday you can buy her a car.

What you do in those six months in between earning

your first paycheck and having to start paying back your loan is critical. If you can set a decent amount of cash aside by the time your first monthly bill arrives, you should use those funds to pay back a good chunk of your loan ASAP. The time I spent saving money in the first six months that I was out of school and earning a paycheck enabled me to be able to pay off my loan within three years. *Time is important here, and you can either make time work for you or against you.* My advice? Make it work for you. If you found a job a little later than you would have liked, and don't have six months to save before your first loan payment is due, all is not lost. Use the time you have- whatever the amount- to the best of your ability. You can still use these overarching principles and apply them to your unique situation; it will just take more effort on your part to make up for lost time, but if you are dedicated, I believe you can do it. Now is the time to put your binge-watching skills to work. If you can binge-watch a season of *House of Cards* in one day, you can do this.

Step 1: Six months to save.

Starting with paycheck numero uno, start putting as much money aside as you can. You have one less monthly payment right now, so don't go blowing it on mounds of guac as I made the case for in the prior chapter. Save any extra money you have (after you've paid all your bills) in your savings account for safe keeping and easy access. If you're able to live with your parents or roommates after graduation, that is an even better way to save money on those bills! A time like this will make you appreciate living with the 'rents again. If free homemade meals and unlimited

TV cable channels aren't incentive enough to keep you sane, just think -it's like you're paying yourself to live with them.

I was able to save a decent amount of money from the time I started my job in June until November, even without having roommates, or moving back in with my parents. So learn from my mistake and think of how much more you can save if you can stand your friends playing loud music while you're trying to sleep, or your parents telling you to take the dog out. You'll be amazed at how much money you can save if you put forth the effort. After one and half years of saving my new income consistently, I had saved nearly $20K!

Step 2: Create a monthly budget.

Just because I was storing money away for the future to pay off my debt, didn't mean I was sitting on my ugly floral couch at home, and it doesn't mean you have to either. This is where having a **budget** can help you. Believe it or not, you can budget in savings and fun. Dollar beer night? Check! New work clothes? Check! You may be surprised to find your new work pants cost less than yoga pants these days- I know I was. Ideally, as soon as you know your starting salary, you should start putting together a monthly budget and include the minimum payment amount for your loan first. Similar to when you start packing for a trip, you need to get the basics, like ~~makeup~~ socks, and ~~hot hair tool weapons~~ underwear, packed before you do anything else.

Next, budget other expenses you will have each month, such as rent, cell phone bill, car payment, and utilities. I know you have experience budgeting how much room you have in your suitcase when packing for vacation. For example, you carefully plan how much space you will need allotted for clothes, toiletries, jewelry, and of course, shoes. Use this packing metaphor on your financial budget. Shoes, much like rent, will take up most of your suitcase real estate. Begin with the big stuff and fixed payment amounts like your rent. Then worry about all the little categories you can squeeze in, like money for groceries and fuel.

After you've accounted for the essentials, don't forget to budget in the fun stuff too, like shopping and going out to dinner! This is like leaving room for those random gifts you'll take back with you, like key chains and shot glasses. I mean, you can never have too many, according to every tourist gift shop. Trust me, if you budget correctly, you won't feel like you're on a budget. After you've paid your bills, stayed within your budget, and saved, the rest is yours to spend however you want! Just don't go too crazy with the tacky tourist gifts.

Having a monthly budget will hold you accountable for saving money towards your student loan payments. It will also help you prepare for the end of those six months when your grace period is over and your loan payments begin. Your friends might be in panic mode thinking they are a victim of identity theft when their card gets declined at happy hour, but you'll be able to save the day and cover their tab, because you were prepared to have your monthly student loan payment taken out of your account. There are tools, such as Mint (**www.mint.com**) that will link directly to your bank account, so you know in real time whether you are on or off track with your budget. You can impress your new boss with your knowledge of exporting spreadsheets, making pivot tables, and graphs ("Oh, that wasn't the right spreadsheet, that was just my simple monthly budget-indexed and color coded!"). Speaking of spreadsheets and indexing, you can find more details about comparing your actual spending with benchmarks in the FAQ section. It's like a report card to see how you're doing, and just like in your school days, you may be shocked by what you see and some adjustments may need to be made.

There are many thoughts, articles, and blogs on ways to budget, so do a little research to see which methods work best for you.

Step 3: Pay a large amount.

Remember when I said after one and half years of saving, I had nearly $20K in the bank? Well, after realizing I had saved enough to put a **down payment** on my own island, I thought I had better put that money to good use instead of letting it sit in a savings account collecting $0.67 in interest each month. One day, I mustered up enough courage and decided to do something crazy- write a $10K check to the federal government. I know better than anyone this could get you 100 pairs of yoga pants, or like 3K cheap beers at dollar beer night, but that $10K check was a game changer. Not only had I never handed over so much cash in my life (and never have again to this day), but I've also never been happier that I did.

All that saving that you do in Step 1 will pay off big time when you use it to pay down a large chunk of your student loan debt. Trust me on this and do it sooner rather than later. I know it's hard handing over most of your savings, all that you've earned from your new job, in one big payment (especially after shredding all your home decor catalogs, and still consuming large amounts of PB & J). But, doing this will actually save you money in the long run. Interest is your friend at a time like this, not your enemy like we talked about back in Chapter 1. You'll pay way less interest because you are using time to your advantage- translation: all the money you save in interest will pay for those expensive sandals you're trying to sneak in your suitcase. Motivated? Yeah, I would be, too.

$10K may be a lot for you. I know I never thought I'd actually see that number in my life! I circled the mailbox for what seemed like 20 minutes, interrogated the mailman, and cried for weeks upon its departure from my hand. Okay, so maybe that's a dramatization, but it was difficult to do! Anything will help here, so don't feel like you have to wait until a certain number is in your bank account. The idea is that you are using money you saved in Step 1 to pay down a portion of your loan as soon as you can. Save, budget, and plan to make a large payment (whatever the amount) on your student loan as early as possible.

Step 4: Pay above your minimum.

You know those overachievers in school? Even though they were irritating when they showed you up in class by actually doing the homework and sitting in the front of the room- you can learn a few things from them. Overachieving, in this instance, will get you the results you want in a faster amount of time. Remember your monthly payment number due on your official student loan plan? Well, if you want to pay your loan off faster and save money in the process, then you're going to need to pay above your minimum monthly payment. What do I mean by that?

I decided that although my monthly bill to the FedLoan Servicing said $332.95, I was going to pay $500.00 a month. And I did. Each month, I paid a minimum of $500.00, 50% as much as what was technically due. The act of writing a check for $500.00, or seeing it debited from your account each month in itself is not that challenging. What IS challenging is choosing to pay $500.00 when you know you aren't required.

Aim to pay +50% of your monthly payment, and pay that amount each month. Factor that number into your monthly budget. If you can't ~~close your suitcase~~ afford to pay that percentage above your minimum, then look for other areas where you can ~~find space~~ cut costs. You may have to look hard, and decide what is really worth keeping. What's more important to you, looking cute in expensive workout wear that you'll sweat in anyway, or not having to pay $400 a month for the rest of your life? And if you really can't do +50% each month, at the very least pay above your minimum!

Step 5: Repeat step 4 until you are debt-free.

Step 5 says everything you need to know in the title. Keep paying above your monthly payment consistently each month. Hold yourself accountable and in no time, you'll be debt-free!

So now you know what you need to do to pay off your student loan and you have an actual plan you can work with (no offense to the Standard Student Loan Plan). If you use your time wisely to store away money, use a budget, make a large payment on your loan early, and continue to pay above your monthly minimum, it won't take you 20 years to pay off that pesky debt. Follow these five steps to financial freedom and if you stick to them and keep your eyes on the prize (a dream vacation or whatever makes you happy), you'll be one of those in the 20% who are living the debt-free life, sipping margaritas on the beach.[14]

---

[14] *The Complex Story of American Debt*. Report. July 2015.

CHAPTER 4

How to Stay on Your Plan to Repayment

What it Takes to Become Debt-Free

So what is it going to take to put this plan into action? By now, I haven't sugar-coated the fact that in order to pay off your student loan debt, it is going to take some serious dedication. But, if you're motivated enough, you can do it. Just like making the decision to get yourself to the gym every ~~other~~ day, it will take making the decision every month to pay more than you owe. You need to realize that depriving yourself now will bring you a debt-free future. Sweating in the gym today = tomorrow's ~~sprinkle donut (guilt free!)~~ stronger you.

Remember when I said my monthly bill to the FedLoan Servicing was $332.95, yet, I decided I was going to pay $500.00 a month? I continued to pay $500.00 each month, knowing I technically didn't have to do that. You don't technically have to work out either, but why do people do it? Certainly, not just to show off their array of yoga pants. They work out because they know the value it has on their long-term health. I know this may be shocking to you, but to actually get the benefits and the results, you're going to have to do the work. You can't be like one of those first-of-year gym-goers who take up all the parking spaces for the month of January, and quits somewhere between the pizza and wings come Super Bowl Sunday.

I'm sure that by now, you've eaten enough pizza and refined carbs for a lifetime, so step away from the high calories snacks and get your steps in to becoming financially fit. Besides, you need to burn off all those PB & J sandwiches and mac and cheese dinners anyway. There will be times when you're challenged and stretched to your limits (think hard breathing and legs shaking like Jell-O). There will be a million temptations to spend your money on things other than your financial freedom, but can you discipline yourself to stick to your budget? Here are some tips for those of you, like me, who may be more inclined to eat the sprinkled donut than to do squats.

Discipline Isn't a Unique Gene; EVERYONE Can Be Disciplined.

To become disciplined in fitness and in life- you just have to do it (or so I'm told every time I put on my gym shoes). It takes doing it over and over again until it becomes a habit and part of your lifestyle. It's easy to tell ourselves that certain people have a gene that makes them more disciplined than others, that these people possess the strength to make it that last mile to finish a marathon and have the will power to never eat an unhealthy carb again (eye roll) – but that's not us. Well, that's simply not true. You'll be surprised at what you can accomplish if you go for it. You don't have to like it at first- you just have to get going and stick to it. That's the difference between those people who finish marathons or never eat cake, and the rest of us. They simply started to take action and make good choices and somewhere around mile 14, discipline found them. If you start somewhere, and keep making good decisions with your money, you can be disciplined in your finances and will see the finish line of being debt-free.

The Beginning is Difficult, Everything that Comes After is Cake.

Why do you think those New Year's Resolution (NYR) gym-goers don't make it past January 31st to meet their fitness goals? Because, the barrier to entry is high, and most people can't see or even get over the barrier. For those who stick with it long enough to make it over their barrier (sleep, ice cream, or TV) they realize the rest is a piece of cake.

What are your barriers to paying off your debt? Think about them, know them, write them on paper, and sleep with them next to you if you must. This is equivalent to your favorite junk food, your kryptonite, whatever your weakness is that will stop you from following your plan to pay off your student loan debt. When you are aware of your weaknesses ahead of time, you can prepare yourself for when you meet them head on.

Half of the battle is not putting yourself in those situations in the first place. Steer clear of the mall if you're worried you'll buy everything in sight. Don't go to the promotions tab in your email if you might see the line of "an extra 10,000 miles on your account if you purchase a flight today!" in your inbox. Do whatever you can to avoid your barriers, but have a plan in place if you run into them unexpectedly, like when your friend suggests you go for ice cream after dinner. We've already gone over the fact that you have the will power to say no to ice cream, and go home instead. So make it easier to say no by arming yourself with lines like: "That kick-boxing class wore me out today, maybe another time."

It's the little choices you make every day, like saying no to ice cream and deciding to go to the gym instead of the mall, that will help you get over the barrier to being in shape financially. It's getting over that first challenge you run into that is the hardest part, and that's where some people give up (aka those NYR gym-goers). Those people who give up don't realize that once you make it over your hurdle, the rest is easy. This is what enables those marathoners to finish their last mile, to stick with it long enough to achieve their goal. On your way to achieving your goal of paying off your student loan debt, you'll have to get past mile 13 first. It will take saying "no" to a 50% off sale or two. But here's a secret: there will be more 50% sales in your future- just after you're debt-free. When you are debt-free, you can spend your money however you want. So get your butt to the gym instead of the mall- you'll thank yourself later.

Visualize Your Destination- Beach Body or Sun Bathing

The key to achieving any goal is to visualize it first. Clear picture = clear motivation. Whether your goal is getting in shape for bikini season, or paying off your debt to afford a beach vacation in the first place, if you paint a picture of what you want your end result to be, you'll be that much more motivated to get there. Do whatever you have to do to keep that picture in your mind for those tough days when you have to do a high jump over your hurdles (50% sales and sprinkled donuts). How will you feel when you pay off your student debt? What will you do with the $500 a month you've been spending on your payment? Got it? Good. Now keep that in your mind every time you see that dreaded number come out of your checking account.

Of course, it's easier said than done to visualize your destination. It's hard to resist when your friends from the shoe warehouse write a letter inviting you to take $20 off your next visit, or when you're at happy hour and your friends are pounding top shelf margaritas. Just like trying to get into beach body shape, give yourself little healthy treats now and then to help you stick to the plan (no one's perfect, right?). It's important to celebrate the successes of the small goals you achieve on the way to becoming debt-free. For example, if you've paid above your minimum monthly student loan payment for four months in a row, then celebrate with getting the expensive wine at a nice dinner with friends, or treating yourself to a pedicure. These little treats will serve as reminders that you've made progress towards your goal, and will serve as a little taste of the sweet freedom that is to come.

The Buddy System Never Fails: Seek Accountability.

Enlist your friends on your journey to becoming debt-free. Isn't that what friends are for? Like making you run that extra mile when you feel like you're about to die, and getting your butt out of bed in the morning when you just want to sleep in? Chances are, we could never do it on our own, but having someone present, cheering us on, and making us try harder, gets us closer to our goal than if we would have done it alone.

Doing anything with a friend makes it more fun. I know what you're thinking: how could paying off debt be fun? Here's some ideas you can do with a friend to save money and have a little fun in the process. It's not rocket science, but if you need some inspiration and motivation, that's why I'm here.

- **Dinner party**- Instead of going out for dinner on the weekend, host a dinner party and invite friends. Make the main dish and invite them to bring the sides. Or, invite a friend over for dinner, and catch up as you learn how to cook a new recipe together.
- **Go for a walk**- Instead of being mistaken for a mall walker by the cops at the mall because you're there so often, go outside and drag a friend with you. Explore your new city, or find some free parks to visit. Added bonus—it burns calories, too!
- **Netflix marathon**- This is my kind of marathon, and my go-to on a weekend night with friends, especially during the cold months of the year. This seems like an obvious one, but did you know your local library will let you check out seasons of shows and recent movies on your card? Unlike your credit card, you can use this card as often as you wish!

- **Find a cheap (or better yet, free) hobby-** Join a gym, learn how to cook or bake, or get into photography- those are just a few ideas. Find ways to spend your time instead of spending all your money.

- **Coffee house-** If you're addicted to those daily lattes in a green and white cup, try inviting a friend over for coffee or tea, instead of meeting at the local coffee house. You could also BYOC on a walk to the park if you're wanting to get out. Or, if you really can't live without your dose of caramel macchiato, put it in your budget!

- **Volunteer-** This one is an easy and free activity that also makes you feel good about yourself and meet new people. Win-win-win, all the way around. Find something you care about or a young professionals group in your city; I'm sure they would love your help and support.

- **Spa day in-** Sometimes you just need a mani/pedi. Instead of dropping $100 every few weeks, get your girlfriends together and do each others' nails while you catch up on your shows.

- **Make it special-** You can keep yourself on track to paying off your student loan by establishing your own set of rules, such as: "I only go out to eat or shopping with friends- never alone." I don't know what tempts you to spend money, but think of those things and create a set of rules around them that will allow you to limit your spending and still allow you to indulge from time to time. It helps if these rules are only done with others, or for special occasions and celebrations. Depriving yourself forever is way too hard and creates room for spending binges! In other words, you can have your cake and eat it, too, but make sure you have a good reason to celebrate!

These are just a few ideas to get you started. There are many more ways you can entice your friends to support you and your decision to get out of debt. It will be more tolerable if you do it together, so use the buddy system you learned in school, and get one of your friends to keep you accountable. Just like enlisting a work out buddy, it will be sure to benefit your friend, too!

Now that you're mentally and physically prepared to pay off your student loan, let's recap:

- You can be disciplined enough to pay above your monthly minimum payment on your loan because you know that it will benefit you in the long run.
- When you start out, it will be hard, but stick with it, and you can make it to the finish line.
- Have a clear picture of your goals- put them on the fridge if you must. What will an extra $500 a month mean for your finances and your life?
- Seek accountability to help get you there. You know that old saying your grandparents would recite? There is strength in numbers!

CHAPTER 5

Extra Income

If All Else Fails, Consider a Side Hustle

As the realities of living costs, taxes, and debt sets in, it's enough to make you wonder if you might need a second job. Ideally, with a full-time position and a salary, you shouldn't need a part-time job on the side. But, if celebrities who make millions have side hustles in the form of perfumes, books, clothing lines, etc., you can, too. Having a second job or source of income could come in handy to supplement your lifestyle, or offset the cost of your student loan payment.

Don't go updating your LinkedIn account just yet, though. Although I didn't have a job in addition to my full-time career, any extra money I had in the form of tax returns, bonuses, and savings, went right to paying off my student loan. Those are good places to start looking for some extra money, in addition to your jean pockets and the washer.

In fact, the one positive thing about the interest you're accumulating on your student loan is that you can deduct it from your taxes. Before you get too excited about the fact that you could be in for a nice tax return come April, commit yourself to put your tax return money back towards your monthly student loan payment. But, of course, use a little chunk of it to treat yourself for making the hard choice. Follow this plan for any extra money you get that you weren't expecting, in addition to extra savings. You'll be glad you did when you can retire from just one job instead of two.

After you've counted all of your extra **assets**, it still may not be enough to get rid of your student loan in the amount of time you'd like. Now, it's time to consider that side hustle. The good news is, you needn't look at your newsfeed long to get inspired.

It seems like everyone has an extra job these days to supplement their salary. It has even crossed my mind. As I read my **W-2** from a previous year and realized I made more in six months at my corporate job than what my annual salary is now at a non-profit, making a little extra cash has become even more appealing. Though I have yet to actually need a second job (due to being debt-free), my entrepreneurial mind is always at work thinking of what I could do in my free time to make money. Why do you think I wrote this book?

Here is a list of things I have come up with so far:

- Write a book
- Become a fitness instructor
- Freelance writer
- Babysitting
- Direct sales rep
- Craft store on Etsy

- Barista
- Flip houses
- Start my own business

If you're serious about paying off your student loan quickly, and your income isn't going to get you there as fast as you would like, think about other ways you could make money. One of my friends recently became a wedding officiant- all it took was a little paperwork and a small fee. You can make people happy on the best day of their life, and make some money. Who says money and happiness don't go hand in hand?

A second source of income doesn't have to mean a second source of sweat and tears. Think about your talents, or what you like to do in your free time, and determine if other people would pay you. A lot of the activities on my list are things I would want to do anyway, and it's a bonus that I could get paid for them. Create a list for yourself, like I did, of the things you like to do that have the potential to be lucrative enough to offset your monthly student loan payment.

If you've always loved photography, try your hand at shooting family photos. If you enjoy hanging out with kids, you could work at children's gym or nanny. If you knit or crochet, make some scarves and sell them online or at your grandma's nursing home. If you like baking, bake the desserts for someone's party. There are plenty of ways you can make a little extra cash and do something you enjoy in the process- people may even thank you for it. Just think, if Kate Hudson didn't have her side hustle selling affordable athletic gear, we would all be destined to forever pay more for yoga pants than dress clothes. Thanks, Kate.

So when the math doesn't add up, don't be overwhelmed. It's not the end of the world; just cut your costs, and go the extra mile by cleaning out your handbags for loose change! If you're really motivated to pay off your loan ahead of schedule, then a side gig might be something you should consider. Who knows, your side job might catapult you into celebrity status.

If you don't land a spot on a reality TV show, now you have a backup plan to becoming a celebrity. All your hard work being disciplined, saving, and going above and beyond, will pay off. After all, celebrities don't get discovered, they are made. They sweat it out it in the gym so they can live an extraordinary life of bliss on the beach. And you can, too.

FINAL THOUGHTS

The statistics on student loan debt can be defeating and overwhelming. Instead of comparing yourself to other people, you can take control of your life and future, and not be controlled by your debt.

By making sacrifices in the short term, I reaped the benefits, and you can, too. I now have my dream job, and I no longer have to worry about a loan payment while I sip margaritas on the beach! Just take one step at a time, and you'll be fine. Remember, progress is most important here.

Again, I never said being part of the 20% of people who live debt-free would be easy, but it'll be worth it.[15] Trust me, it will be worth eating your weight in peanut butter when you finally get that letter saying your loan is paid in full. By then, you won't have to wait for a rose, because you'll be financially self-sufficient.

When that happens, I hope to hear from you. I want to hear how you achieved the life of your dreams.

-Angela

---

[15] *The Complex Story of American Debt*. Report. July 2015.

GLOSSARY

401(k) -

How your employer helps you to plan for retirement. Don't worry just yet if you don't see a 401(k) on your organization's website. They might have a similar plan known as 401 3B, or 457. Don't get these confused with your apartment number, a 401(k) is just the most common retirement contribution plans. No need to freak out that you'll never be able to retire if your employer doesn't offer any retirement plan. You can plan for retirement on your own, too, so you won't miss watching your future grandkids grow up.

You can start putting money in your 401(k) or company-offered retirement plan after your first day on the job. Each organization has a different timeline. Check the earliest you can start, to take full advantage. The earlier you start, the more you'll make, even if you contribute less over time. Makes no sense, right? Yeah, that's what I think too, but that's what I learned from my dad and my math professor in school. And don't forget about those matching funds that may be available!

I could write a whole other book on investing for retirement (and I just might). So we've covered as much as you need to know to get you started. Do be aware that any money you put into a 401(k) is pre-taxed, though, which means the money comes out of your paycheck before the government gets to take their cut. This also means if you withdraw funds before you retire, there will be a penalty (of course) in the form of a charge ON TOP of being taxed. Not a good idea. Say so long to any money you put in the account, you'll see it again when you have grey hair and wrinkles. It doesn't sound like fun now, but you'll be glad you did.

APR (Annual Percentage Rate)-

Just a fancy way of saying "interest" that's expressed annually. Use this acronym when you want to impress your friends.

Assets-

Another fancy term for anything you own that could produce some value. Make sure to protect your assets.

Budget-

In this case, not a transportation service. It's your game plan for how to manage your income and control your expenses.

Consolidate-

The act of combining your student loans (if you have multiple) into one monthly payment. Now, if you could just consolidate your job applications…

Credit Card-

A magical card that lets you pay for things, no matter how much money you have or don't have!

Credit Score-

Your adult report card that determines your life after school. All that time you wasted in school worrying about your grades when you should have been worrying about this score. This test measures your trustworthiness to handle money. You want a perfect score on this exam- a 720 or higher.

Direct PLUS Loan -

Your school has to be in this after-school program for you to be eligible. You must be working on a higher degree (at least half the time), or be the parent of an undergrad student going at least part-time.

Direct Subsidized Loan-

The government pays your interest on this loan while you're in school or in the grace period. It's like a free pass. Remember those from grade school?

Direct Unsubsidized Loan-

Watch out, because fees apply here. Regardless of your martial or loan status, you'll have to pay the charge on this loan during AND after school.

Down Payment-

This is your first down with more ~~yardage~~ payments to go for the completion of the ~~play~~ loan.

Employee Stock Purchase Plan (ESPP)-

If your organization has one of these, that means you get a discount on their stock. It doesn't sound as exciting as a discount at your favorite clothing store, but if you work for a company that is uber (no pun intended) competitive and on the up and up (think Apple and Google in the early 2000s), you could cash in your stock to buy a yacht one day.

FAFSA-

The dreaded paperwork to apply for a federal student loan every year you attended school. Bet you're glad you'll never have to fill out that again! Now, you just have your annual tax forms to look forward to.

Federal Perkins Loan-

These are low interest loans -think clearance sale of student loans. Before you go wishing your loan had been on sale, these loans are for those who need the discount. Not all schools will have this one available, but if yours does, you'll be saying thank you by paying them your loan payment (which they'll receive through a loan servicer) instead of the government.

FICO® -

It's the most popular credit score in class. Unlike the posers who will claim to give you your credit score, this is the real deal. FICO®-1, All other credit scores –0.

Fully Vested -

This isn't the term for when cool weather hits and you survey your collection of puffy vests taking up room in your closet. This is in reference to your 401(k). Any money you contribute into your company 401(k) is yours. The organization you work for may contribute matching funds for anything you contribute up to a certain amount. This is a benefit for you, and also an incentive to storing away cash for when your hips can't shake it like they used to and you would rather garden all day than work. Well, the money that your organization matches "vests" over time as money you get to keep. After a period of four to five years, you get to keep that money from your organization if you choose to part ways. If you part your separate ways before the time period is up, then you may only get a percentage of those matched funds, or none at all. So I highly recommend you ask this in an interview as you get closer to a final offer. Plus, they'll be impressed you've heard about it and know what it means.

Grace Period-

Remember free period back in high school? Well, this is one period you don't want to blow off. The government gives you a freebie for six months on your loan, but be careful as charges may apply! Refer back to Chapter 1B if you need a refresher.

Interest -

Unlike when you paid back your parents growing up, when you borrow money from anyone, they charge you extra for having it. This is the case for student loans, and anyone you borrow money from who isn't your blood relative.

Interest is calculated in the form a percentage on the original loan amount. This is why it's so important to pay back your student loan ASAP, because the earlier you do, the less interest you'll pay.

The type of loan you have and if Congress was having a good year when you received your loan is what matters here.

If you ask me, this interest is anything but simple. To calculate the formula, you'll need to know which months have 31 days, and which have less (also when you made your last payment). Think back to your grade school rhymes if you aren't near a calendar. This is like one of those algebra problems where you'll need to solve for X before you solve for Y. In this case your "X" is the Interest Rate Factor found below. Here's the formula written out that you can find on the FSA website.

Simple daily interest formula:
Outstanding principal balance
x number of days since last payment
interest rate factor
= Interest amount

Interest Rate Factor-

Divide the interest rate on your loan by 365 and you've got it.

IRA (Individual Retirement Account)-

Remember when I said you can save for retirement on your own, too? Well, an IRA is how you do that. Put this on your must-have list. I recommend you have one of these in addition to your 401(k) or employer retirement fund -and the sooner the better. Why? Because of the impact of compounding. If you're having terrible flashbacks to using the time value of money formula in school, it may be the only bit of education worth your student loan payment. Again, I have to save something to write a second book about, so all you need to know right now is get one (I recommend a Roth) and start putting money in it ASAP. You'll be on your way to retiring at 55 when your friends who didn't follow this advice are still working post-dentures.

Loan Disbursement-

This is what it's called when the government releases your loan funds. Don't treat these funds like paper money and you'll be fine.

Loan Forgiveness-

The cancelation of all or part of what you owe if you work for qualified employers, such as public schools, the military, and non-profits. It's the government's way of saying thank-you for your service to 'mercia and its future.

Loan Servicers-

They collect your payments on behalf of the lender. In this case- the federal government. Too bad they don't have an app for that.

Pension Plan-

Another form of your employer helping you in retirement. I know it's hard to imagine, but back in the day when your parents or your grandparents were working, it was common for them to work for one organization for 30 years. I know, right!? These were the days before the cell phones diminished our attention span to four seconds. When their organization had a pension plan, they got a pretty much guaranteed monthly paycheck in retirement. Sound nice, right? Sorry, these are nearly out of style. If your future employer still has one, it might be worth sticking around for 30 years. The more time you serve, the more money in that retirement paycheck.

Principal-

The original amount you borrowed. Some things are better left in the original state: loans, the National Parks, and chocolate.

Stafford Loans-

Voted the most likely to succeed, this loan is the most common. AKA, Subsidized and Unsubsidized. Just another name for your loan, as if you weren't confused already.

W-2-

Not a cover band of U2's music. A W-2 is like a report card you get in January. It tells you how you much you earned last year. Luckily, on this report card there are no grades, and even better, it will help you out with your taxes.

FREQUENTLY ASKED QUESTIONS:

Validated by experts; written for you

Credit:

Expert: Britt Scearce, Business Development at local credit union

How can I check my credit score?

There are a lot of credit scoring models out there. More often than not, your credit card company will give you your score for free (I know mine does), so check there first! A FICO® score is the most popular score in town that most lenders use. Go to Myfico.com to get yours today, but be aware they will charge you like Netflix does for monitoring plan, or you can pay once to obtain your score.

What makes up a FICO® score?

You'll be judged in five areas that together make up your FICO® score found in your credit report. Check out the following:

- Payment History – 35%

- Total Amounts Owed – 30%
- Length of Credit History – 15%
- New Credit – 10%
- Type of Credit in Use – 10%

A credit score of 720 and above gets you the best that money can buy.

What can I do to improve my score if I don't like what I see?

Don't worry, not all is lost. You can make-up this exam by doing a few things to earn extra credit. However, it will require some time on your part.

Step 1: Make sure all of your accounts are up to date!

If you have any past dues in your inbox, get to work paying them off. It's all about consistency here. Stick to paying at least the minimum on your accounts for a year, and your score will increase significantly.

Step 2: Go back through your credit report and check for any mistakes.

If there are any, use your newly learned negotiation skills to take it up with the man.

Step 3: If you run into a little trouble, ask for a deadline extension.

The dog ate my homework excuse won't work here, but you have had practice asking your teachers for extra time, so ask one more time here. While you're at it, get your creditors to clear your history if you've have a run in or two in the past of not paying on your accounts. You've seen the errors in your ways, and made strides to follow after the overachiever in class, but your record may still be working against you. You can try to negotiate a clean slate.

Fix your mistakes over time and aim high (by asking for a higher credit limit). Remember, the higher the degree of difficulty, and sticking to your payments= a better score.

When should I get my first credit card, if I don't already have one?

As I mentioned in Chapter 3: proceed with caution. However, the length of time credit has been established is 15% of the FICO® credit scoring model, so establishing accounts ASAP helps to start building a history of responsibly managed credit. If your parents haven't kicked you out yet, it's a good time to ask for one more favor- to be added as authorized user on their well-established account. If that's a no go, then open a secured credit card at your bank or credit union. And remember, handle with care!

Why shouldn't I cancel my other credit cards?

This seems unproductive, but trust me, it could do more damage than good. Don't close any credit card that still has a balance. Why? Because, if you do, your total available credit and credit limit are reported as $0. In my experience,

$0 is never a good thing. It will appear to people (like lenders) looking at your record that you've maxed out on your accounts, which can be bad news for your credit score. Bottom line: do not close out all your credit cards. Keep at least one open and use it responsibly. And if you do want to close an account, make sure it's not the one you've had in your wallet the longest. These people really like history.

Job:

Expert: Sherry Sims, HR professional and Founder of Black Career Women's Network

What starting salary should I expect?

Do your homework on this one so you know what to expect when you get an offer of employment. Ask your professors, look online, or ask your sorority sister who graduated last year. Check websites like Payscale.com and the U.S. Bureau of Labor Statistics, or industry journals and resources. Look for a range of what you can expect to earn your first year out of school. Your starting salary will be based on how much experience and education is required for the position based on the industry and market rate for your city. Remember to account for the cost of living in the area. For example, the cost of living in San Fran is higher than Cincinnati, OH, so salaries should reflect that as well.

Should I negotiate salary for my first job?

Yes, especially if you have unique talents, skill sets, education, or certifications that you know will set you apart from your peers. Stand out from the crowd, and stand up for yourself!

Where are the best places to search for a job after college?

Searching within your network is the best place to start. Join some LinkedIn groups and start introducing yourself. Get your network on and go to networking events in your city or on campus. Flattery will always open doors-ask for an informal interview or job shadow opportunity from the new connections you make.

How can I perfect my resume?

Monster.com is a great resource for job searching techniques, resume samples, and interview questions. Don't have a resume? They have you covered with resume templates you can download and use for any industry.

Loans:

Why did I receive less money than I actually borrowed?

Good question! If you're looking through your loan documents and the math doesn't add up, that's because in addition to the interest you pay for having borrowed money-you get charged a fee. Think of the federal government as an ATM, you took cash out from that wasn't your bank. It's like the reverse of getting out a $20 but being charged

$23. And guess what? You'll have to pay back the $23 full amount you borrowed.

Why do I have to pay back my student loan if I didn't even finish school?

The easy answer? So you don't show up on the government's naughty list. Unfortunately, the federal government has a no full return policy. If you use it, you pay for it. That'll make you think twice before dropping out of school, thinking you're the next Bill Gates. But if you are following in his footsteps, I hope you make it big sooner rather than later because you'll be paying back what you used.

What is the difference between a Federal and Private Loan?

If you've been paying attention, you'll know Federal Loans are passed out by the government. Private loans are given by your bank, credit union, school, or through the state you live in. If you have a private loan, it's more likely that your loan will have accrued interest while you were sitting in class. Chances are, it's at varying rates that could be higher than what Congress determined that year. These are just a few of the differences. The bad news is, whether you have a Federal or Private loan- you still have to pay it back.[16]

---

[16] "How to Repay Your Loans." *Federal Student Aid*, last modified July 30, 2017

How do I save money during the six months of my grace period? And how much should I save?

If you're not spending your newly-earned cash decking out your new apartment or throwing large parties like the ones you had in school-you won't find this difficult to accomplish. Watch your spending in the areas I went over in Chapter 2, and watch your bank account climb! Chances are, you've never made this amount of money before. After pinching yourself a few times, remind yourself that you had lived on less up until now, so you can manage continuing that lifestyle a little longer. When the grace period is over, you'll have a good chunk of change to make a "down payment" on your loan. Make it a game to see how much you can save in the six-month grace period. Create little rewards along the way for milestones you hit- $1K, $5, $10K! Like I said in Chapter 3, the amount you have after the six months are up is progress made. It's unique to each persons' finances, so this is one answer to the test I can't give you. My example was $10K. By taking these steps, you'll karate chop the amount you'll pay in interest, and be on your way to purchasing flights for that island getaway!

Personal Finances:

Expert: Brad Felix, CFA and Investment Specialist

How do I make a budget?

Creating a budget can seem like a daunting task, but it doesn't have to be. If you download an app on your phone, you can have your budget at your fingertips before you go reaching for your credit card. A little effort up-front will allow you to quickly and easily analyze your budget in the future. Unfortunately, creating and reviewing your budget is something that can't be completed once, just like "saving as" on your resume and doing your taxes. In order to be effective, a budget must be regularly reviewed and adjusted. Follow these instructions from my financial advisor, Brad, that fully explain how to make a budget.

Step 1: Capture your data.

You're a pro at capturing the moment on Instagram, so use your talent to capture a snapshot of how you spend your money. Brad recommends using an aggregating (fancy term for collecting or computing) service like Mint.com.

Mint will help you by automatically capturing and categorizing your expenses for any accounts that you link to their site. While Mint does a great job capturing the data, sometimes it does a poor job of categorizing expenses. Translation: they don't always use the best hashtag to describe your financial picture. By going through your expenses and correctly categorizing your expenses, you'll have a much clearer picture of where your money is going.

Step 2: Benchmark.

Now that you have your spending categorized, how do you know what you should be spending on things like rent and groceries, in relation to your income? All it takes is a little multiplication and division to figure this out. So dust off your math skills once again, and begin by multiplying your paycheck out for the month. This will give you your monthly take home pay, aka your after-tax income. Next, divide your total expenses in each category by your monthly take home pay. This will give you a percentage for each category; you can then compare with a number of different spending benchmarks (Google this or use the resources listed under the next question) to see if you're over-or-under spending relative to a "healthy budget." Let's say for example, I currently spend 10% of my monthly income on clothes, and my spending benchmark says I should be spending 4% (what? only 4%?!). Now I'm aware I'm overspending on clothes, and should ask my roommate to borrow a dress instead of buying one.

What are good resources on budgeting?

As mentioned above, there are a number of different sites that give budgeting frameworks. Check out the U.S Bureau of Labor Statistics again, but this time for budgets instead of job salaries. They provide a budget based upon the averages of its Consumer Expenditure Survey. Another popular source is Financial Peace University which offers guidelines for spending based upon certain categories. There are many other individual sources, as well as a few broad frameworks like the "50/30/20" budget, which advocates spending 50% of your income on essentials like utilities and fuel, 30% on personal and 20% on savings. To recap, a lot of people want to help you with your budget, so pick one that you can work with and stick with it!

Should I get a financial advisor? Why do I need one?

I say a hard yes on this one. If you can't afford one right away, you'll be fine with these budgeting guidelines to get you started. Keep in mind, we have coaches for our fitness, why wouldn't we need a coach for our finances as well? They can help create specific financial ~~fitness~~ goals, build investment portfolios ~~muscles~~ to reach specific goals, and offers guidance ~~motivation~~ for saving. Paying for professional financial services allows you to focus on other parts of your life (like happy hour), and provides peace of mind that your money is working for you!

What should I look for in a financial advisor?

You should look for a fee-only, fiduciary advisor. One of the most important things to ask your advisor is how they are compensated for their services. Similar to how you can ask about money on an interview (unlike a date) this is a rare occasion, so I suggest you take full advantage. A "fee-only" advisor receives no commissions from products they sell, meaning their only compensation comes directly from you. A "fiduciary" advisor is legally obligated to act in your best interest - it's a higher standard of care than someone who only provides advice that is "suitable" for someone in your situation. In summary, look for someone who is paid by you and works in your best interest.

NOTES

1 Powell, Farran. "10 Student Loan Facts College Grads Need to Know." *U.S. News*, May 9, 2016, www.usnews.com/education/best-colleges/paying-for-college/slideshows/10-student-loan-facts-college-grads-need-to-know.

2 Lopez, Mark Hugo, and Ana Gonzalez-Barrera. "Women's College Enrollment Gains Leave Men Behind." *Pew Research Center*, March 6, 2014, www.pewresearch.org/fact-tank/2014/03/06/womens-college-enrollment-gains-leave-men-behind/.

3 Dickler, Jessica. "College Debt Weighs More Heavily on Women than on Men." *CNBC*, CNBC, January 25, 2017, www.cnbc.com/2017/01/25/women-carry-bigger-burden-of-student-loan-debt-than-men.html.

4 Dickler, Jessica. "College Debt Weighs.."

5 Friedman, Zack. "Student Loan Repayment: The Hottest Employee Benefit Of 2017." *Forbes*, Forbes Magazine, February 2, 2017, www.forbes.com/sites/zackfriedman/2016/12/19/student-loan-repayment-benefit/#2f892271d6fe.

6 *The Complex Story of American Debt*. Report. July 2015. www.pewtrusts.org/~/media/assets/2015/07/reach-of-debt-report_artfinal.pdf?la=en.

7 Berman, Jillian. "America's Student-Loan Debt Growing $2,726 Every Second." *MarketWatch*, January 30, 2016, www.marketwatch.com/story/every-second-americans-get-buried-under-another-3055-in-student-loan-debt-2015-06-10.

8 Bidwell, Allie. "Student Loan Expectations: Myth vs. Reality." *U.S. News & World Report*, U.S. News & World Report, October

7, 2014, www.usnews.com/news/blogs/data-mine/2014/10/07/student-loan-expectations-myth-vs-reality.

9 Onink, Troy. "Use These 8 Loans To Pay For College." *Forbes*, Forbes Magazine, June 1, 2016, www.forbes.com/sites/troyonink/2013/01/22/use-these-8-loans-to-pay-for-college/2/.

10 "How to Repay Your Loans." *Federal Student Aid*, last modified July 30, 2017, studentaid.ed.gov/sa/repay-loans.

11 Bidwell, Allie. "Student Loan Expectations: Myth vs. Reality."

12 12 "Student Loan Repayment Estimator." *Repayment Estimator*, studentloans.gov/myDirectLoan/mobile/repayment/repaymentEstimator.action#view-repayment-plans.

13 *The Complex Story of American Debt*. Report. July 2015.

14 *The Complex Story of American Debt*. Report. July 2015.

15 *The Complex Story of American Debt*. Report. July 2015.

16 "How to Repay Your Loans." *Federal Student Aid*, last modified July 30, 2017

ABOUT THE AUTHOR

A Pure Michigan native (and Western Michigan University graduate), Angela currently resides in Cincinnati, OH, where she lives with roommates, so she can afford designer handbags and traveling. If she isn't writing, she's watching a Hallmark Movie with a bowl of popcorn, surrounded by fall-scented candles-no matter the season. If this whole writing thing doesn't work out, she hopes to pursue a full-time career naming nail polish colors, and given the choice, she would rather consume Brussels sprouts than cake.

Printed in the United States
By Bookmasters